Shapes

David Kirkby

RIGBY
INTERACTIVE
LIBRARY

Designed by The Point
Cover design by Pinpoint Design
Printed in the United States of America

00 99 98 97 96
10 9 8 7 6 5 4 3 2 1

Library of Congress Cataloging-in-Publication Data
Kirkby, David, 1943–
    Shapes / David Kirkby.
       p. cm. — (Math live)
    Includes index.
    Summary: Introduces elementary geometric concepts along with simple activities and calculations.
    ISBN 1-57572-041-8 (library)
    1. Geometry—Juvenile literature. [1. Geometry.] I. Title.
II. Series: Kirkby, David, 1943– Math live.
QA445.5.K57 1996
516—dc20   95–20570
                                      CIP
                                        AC

Acknowledgments
The author and publisher wish to acknowledge, with thanks, the following photographic sources:
Hutchison, p. 14; David Muscroft, p. 42c; ALLSPORT/S. Bruty, p. 12; Ace Photo Agency, p. 12; Photo Resources, p. 22; Courtesy Zanussi Ltd, p. 23t; Zefa, pp. 32, 38, 39; Marcus Alexander, p. 42b; Roger Scruton, pp. 18, 19, 24; Courtesy of Fired Earth, p. 14b; Trevor Clifford, pp. 23c, 25.

The publishers would also like to thank the following for the kind loan of equipment:
NES Arnold Ltd; Polydron International Ltd.

> **Note to the Reader**
> In this book some words are printed in **bold** type. This indicates that the word is listed in the glossary on page 44. The glossary gives a brief explanation of words that may be new to you.

CONTENTS

1. TWO DIMENSIONS AND THREE DIMENSIONS   4

2. POLYGONS   6

3. TRIANGLES   8

4. TYPES OF TRIANGLES   10

5. RECTANGLES   12

6. SQUARES   14

7. PARALLELOGRAMS & RHOMBUSES   16

8. TRAPEZOIDS   18

9. QUADRILATERALS   20

10. CIRCLES   22

11. PARTS OF CIRCLES   24

12. POLYHEDRA   26

13. CUBES   28

14. NETS OF CUBES   30

15. RECTANGULAR PRISMS   32

16. PYRAMIDS   34

17. OTHER TYPES OF PRISMS   36

18. CONES AND CYLINDERS   38

19. TETRAHEDRA   40

20. SPHERES AND HEMISPHERES   42

GLOSSARY   44

INDEX   46

ANSWERS   47

Two-dimensional (2-D) shapes are flat and can be drawn on paper. We often call them **plane shapes**.

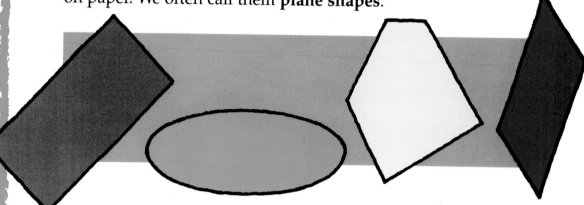

Here are some drawings of two-dimensional shapes. *Do you know any of their names?*

You can measure how long they are and how wide they are. You cannot measure how thick they are. Two-dimensional shapes have length and width. The length and width are their two dimensions.

The straight lines which are used to draw a shape are called its sides. Most two-dimensional shapes have straight sides, but some have curved sides, like the oval shape above.

The corner of a shape is called a **vertex**. If we are talking about more than one vertex, we describe them as **vertices**.

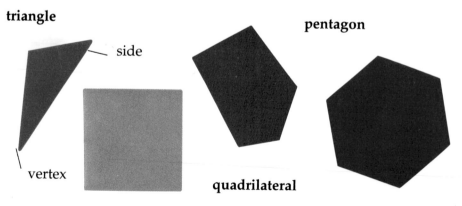

triangle

side

vertex

pentagon

quadrilateral

hexagon

The triangle has 3 sides and 3 vertices.
How many sides and vertices do the other shapes have?

Three-dimensional (3-D) shapes have thickness as well as length and width. We often call them solid shapes.

FACTBOX			
	Length	**Width**	**Thickness**
2-D shapes	✓	✓	✗
3-D shapes	✓	✓	✓

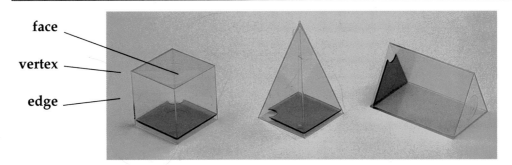

face

vertex

edge

The corners of three-dimensional shapes are also called vertices. The flat part of the shapes are called faces, and the straight lines around them, which join the vertices, are called edges. The pyramid has 5 vertices, 5 faces, and 8 edges.

Can you say how many vertices, faces, and edges the other shapes above have?

So the two-dimensional shapes have vertices and sides, and the three-dimensional shapes have vertices, faces, and edges.

FACTBOX				
	Side	**Vertex**	**Edge**	**Face**
2-D shapes	✓	✓	✗	✗
3-D shapes	✗	✓	✓	✓

TO DO

A Swiss mathematician, Leonard Euler, found a rule for three-dimensional shapes. He said that if you count the number of vertices, faces, and edges, then these totals fit the rule:

vertices + faces = edges + 2.

Check to see if this is true.

POLYGONS

A **polygon** is a two-dimensional shape with straight sides. Polygons have special names based on their number of sides.

 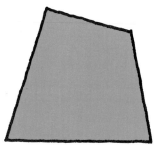  

triangle   **quadrilateral**   **pentagon**   **hexagon**

FACTBOX		
Name	**Sides**	**Vertices**
Triangle	3	3
Quadrilateral	4	4
Pentagon	5	5
Hexagon	6	6
Heptagon	7	7
Octagon	8	8
Nonagon	9	9
Decagon	10	10

Can you name each of these shapes?

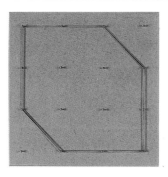 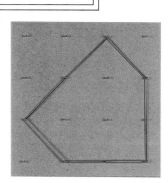

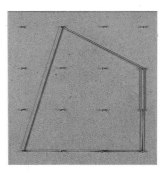 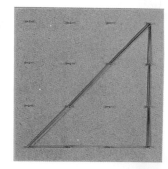

6

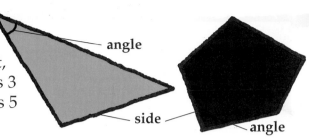

When two sides of a polygon meet, they make an **angle**. A triangle has 3 sides and 3 angles. A pentagon has 5 sides and 5 angles.

The sides sometimes meet at a wide angle, and sometimes meet at a narrow angle. Polygons can have some sides of equal length, and can have some angles of equal size.

If all the sides of a polygon are the same length, and all its angles are the same size it is called a **regular polygon**. If not, it is called an **irregular polygon**.

What do you call a regular four-sided polygon?

TO DO

Make some polygon knots.

To make a pentagonal knot:
• start with a long strip of paper
• fold it loosely as shown
• pull at the two ends.

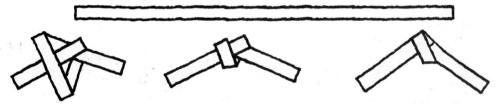

To make a hexagonal knot:
• start with two long strips of paper
• fold them as shown below
• intertwine them and pull the two ends of both strips.

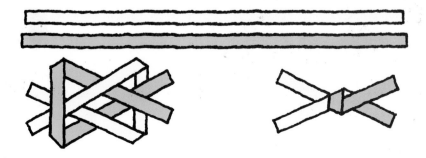

③ TRIANGLES

A **triangle** is a two-dimensional polygon with 3 sides. If an object is shaped like a triangle, we describe its shape as triangular.

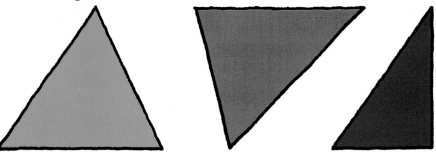

We see triangular shapes all around us.

Many road signs are triangular. There is even a musical instrument called a triangle.

Some roofs have triangular shapes.
Can you see any in this picture?

CHALLENGE

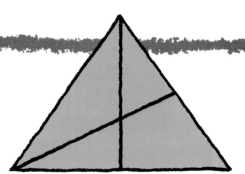

There are 8 triangles in this drawing. Can you find them?

Can you draw a shape that has 12 triangles?

TO DO

The Triangle Game

You need 9 counters.
Start by placing a counter on every spot except one.

To move, jump one counter over another, along the line to the empty spot beyond. The jumped counter is removed.

Continue until you are unable to move. Then add up all the numbers that are not covered by a counter. This is your score.

Play several games.
What is your best score?

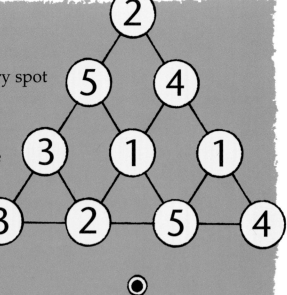

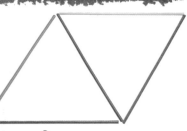

CHALLENGE

You need a set of 12 straws.
Here is how to make 2 triangles using 5 straws.

Can you:
- make 2 triangles with 6 straws?
- make 3 triangles with 7 straws?
- make 3 triangles and make 4 triangles with 9 straws?
- make 4 triangles with 10 straws?
- make 5 triangles with 11 straws?
- make 4 triangles and make 5 triangles with 12 straws?

TYPES OF TRIANGLES

A triangle that has all 3 sides the same length is called an **equilateral triangle.**
If the 3 sides are the same length, it follows that all 3 angles must also be the same size.

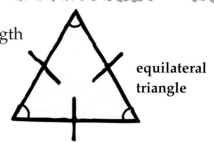

equilateral triangle

To show that the sides are the same length, we draw one short line across each of the equal sides, or sometimes we draw two short lines on each side.

To show that angles are all the same size, we draw one arc across each equal angle, or sometimes we draw two arcs across each. To show that an angle is a right angle, we complete a small square inside the angle.

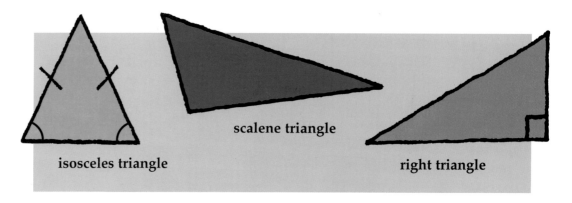

scalene triangle

isosceles triangle

right triangle

Isosceles triangles have 2 sides the same length**.**
They have 2 equal angles. These are the angles at the feet of the equal sides. The sides of **scalene triangles** are all of different lengths. A triangle that has a right angle is called a **right triangle**. This factbox summarizes the properties.

FACTBOX		Number of Equal Sides	Number of Equal Angles	Right Angle
Equilateral		3	3	0
Isosceles		2	2	1 possible
Scalene		0	0	1 possible
Right		0 or 2 possible	2 possible	1

TO DO

Make an equilateral triangle from a paper circle.

 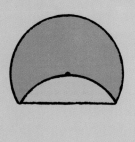 

Start with a paper circle. Mark its center.
- Fold from any point to the center.
- Fold to the center again, from one end of the fold.
- Then fold the last part, and you have made an equilateral triangle.

CHALLENGE

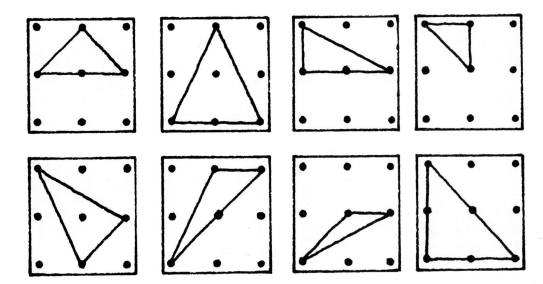

These are the 8 different triangles that can be made on a 3 x 3 pinboard.

How many of the triangles can you name?
How many triangles can you make on a 4 x 4 pinboard?

RECTANGLES

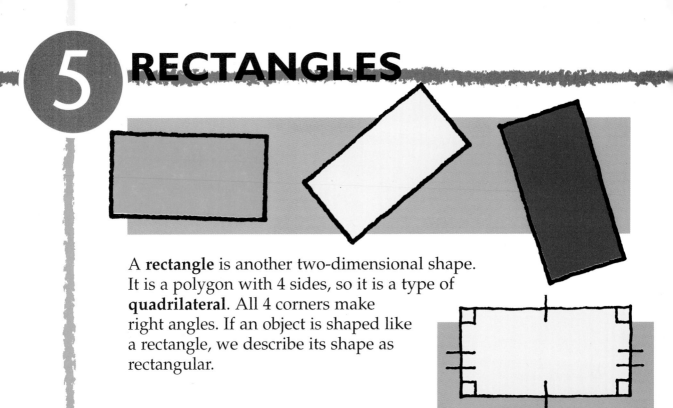

A **rectangle** is another two-dimensional shape. It is a polygon with 4 sides, so it is a type of **quadrilateral**. All 4 corners make right angles. If an object is shaped like a rectangle, we describe its shape as rectangular.

CHALLENGE

Many sports fields have marked rectangles. How many rectangles can you see on this tennis court?

There are many rectangular shapes to be seen, both inside and outside our houses. How many can you see in this picture?

The longer pair of sides measure the length of the rectangle. The shorter pair of sides measure the width of the rectangle. This rectangle is 3 inches wide and 5 inches wide. We say its size is 3 by 5.

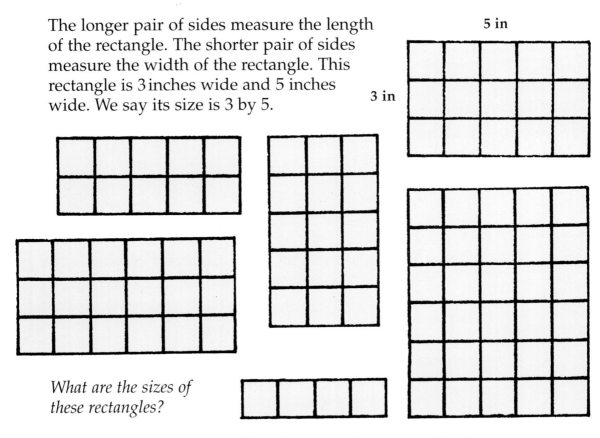

What are the sizes of these rectangles?

Note that a 3 by 5 rectangle is the same shape as a 5 by 3 rectangle.

TO DO

Make some 2 by 1 rectangles, cut from cardboard.

Investigate how many different ways you can place four of them inside a 2 by 4 rectangle. Here are two ways:

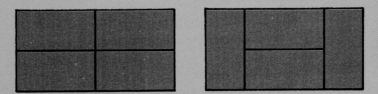

Can you find any more?
Find different ways of placing five inside a 2 by 5 rectangle.

SQUARES

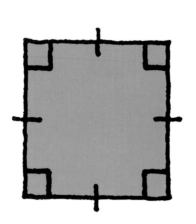
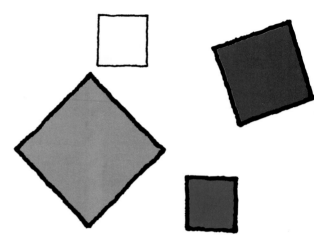
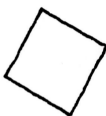

A **square** is a special rectangle, so it is another type of quadrilateral. It has 4 sides, but they are all the same length. Because a square is a rectangle, the 4 corners are right angles.

Many towns have a square space in their center known as the town square. Markets are often held in these squares, one day a week.

Tiles and paving stones are usually square-shaped because they fit neatly together.

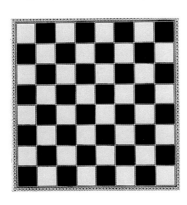

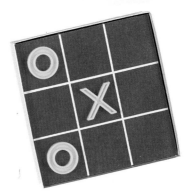

Many games are played on square-shaped boards.
How many small squares are there on the chessboard?

CHALLENGE

There are 14 squares in this 3 by 3 square.
Can you find them?

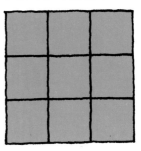

TO DO

How can you make a square when you cannot
measure the sides?

 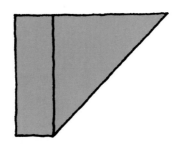  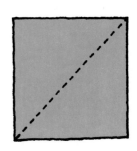

- Start with a rectangular piece of paper.
- Fold one corner so that it meets the other side.
- Draw a straight line along the edge.
- Open out the paper, and cut along the straight line.
- You now have a square piece of paper.

PARALLELOGRAMS & RHOMBUSES

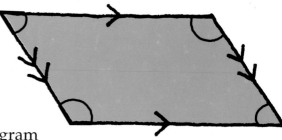

A **parallelogram** is a two-dimensional shape with 4 sides. Rectangles and squares are parallelograms with 4 right angles.

The opposite sides of a parallelogram are the same length and parallel to each other. The pairs of opposite angles are also equal. To show that lines are parallel, we draw an arrow pointing in the same direction on each parallel line. If we need to show another set of parallel lines, we draw two arrows on each line.

This kind of parallelogram can be made by "squashing" a rectangle.

 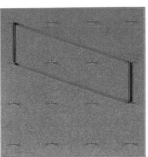  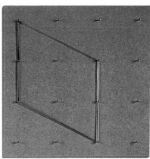

TO DO

Draw a pattern of parallelograms.

- Draw two straight lines on each edge of a ruler.
- Slide the ruler down to draw another parallel line, and so on.
- Turn the ruler so that it crosses the set of parallel lines, and use the same method to draw another set of parallel lines.

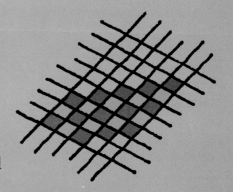

Make a pattern by coloring parallelograms.

A **rhombus** is a special parallelogram. Its 4 sides are all the same length. Both the rhombus and the parallelogram are examples of quadrilaterals because they are polygons with 4 sides.

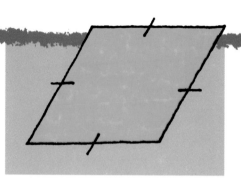

A square is a rhombus. You can make a different kind of rhombus by squashing a square, just as you can make a different kind of parallelogram by squashing a rectangle.

 ## CHALLENGE

- Start with a rectangle.
- Mark a point on the top edge, then draw two lines as shown.
- Cut out the three pieces.

Can you arrange the pieces to make a parallelogram?
Then can you make a different parallelogram?
What other shapes can you make?

8 TRAPEZOIDS

A **trapezoid** is a two-dimensional shape with 4 sides. It is another type of quadrilateral.

The parallelogram and rhombus have two pairs of parallel sides, while the trapezoid has one pair of opposite parallel sides.

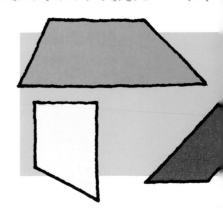

Many roof tops have sides that are trapezoid-shaped.
How many trapezoids can you see in the photograph?

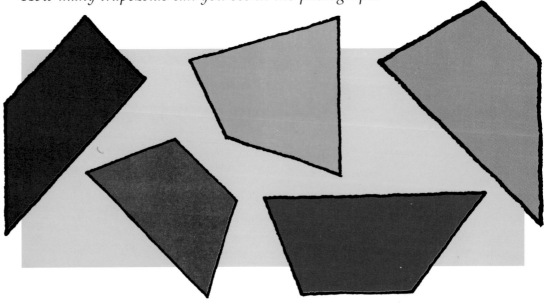

Which of these five shapes is not a trapezoid?
Which are the parallel sides of the four trapezoids?

If you look carefully, there are lots of trapezoid shapes in this gate. There are some that are shaped like this, which are called **right angle trapezoids** because two of the angles are right angles.

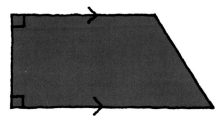

This trapezoid is called an **isosceles trapezoid** because its non-parallel sides are the same length.

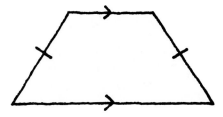

CHALLENGE

- Start with two equally sized squares of cardboard.
- Mark the mid-point of the side of one of the squares. Join it to an opposite corner.
- Cut along the line, so that you now have three pieces, labelled A, B, and C.

By joining the pieces together, can you make a trapezoid using
– A and B
– B and C
– A and C
– A, B, and C?

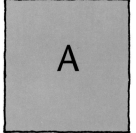

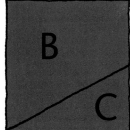

9 QUADRILATERALS

Any polygon that has 4 sides is called a **quadrilateral.**

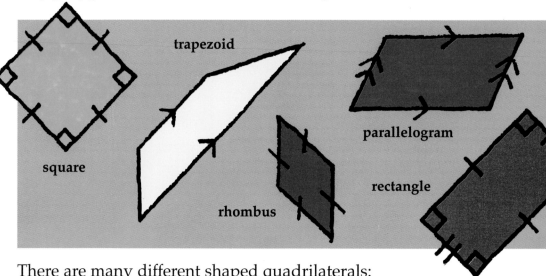

There are many different shaped quadrilaterals:
- a **parallelogram**, which has two pairs of opposite parallel sides
- a **rectangle**, a parallelogram whose opposite sides are the same length and whose angles are all right angles
- a **square**, which is the special rectangle whose 4 sides are all the same length
- a **rhombus**, which is the special parallelogram whose 4 sides are all the same length (a square is a rhombus)
- a **trapezoid**, which has one pair of parallel sides.

A **kite** is another type of quadrilateral. It has two pairs of equal sides.

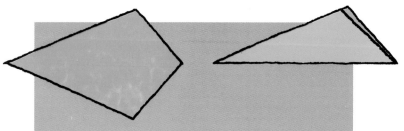

It can be folded in half to make two identical triangles.

When you draw the diagonals of a kite they always meet at right angles, and divide the kite into four right angle triangles.

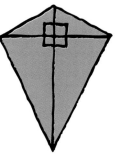

Which of these are not quadrilaterals?
What are the names of the quadrilaterals?

 CHALLENGE

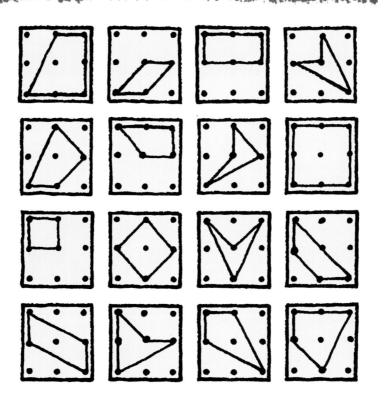

There are 16 different quadrilaterals that can be made on a
3 x 3 pinboard. How many of the quadrilaterals can you
name?

CIRCLES

A **circle** is a plane shape. It is a curved line with every point on the line exactly the same distance from a fixed point. The fixed point is called the center of the circle. If an object is shaped like a circle, we say it is circular.

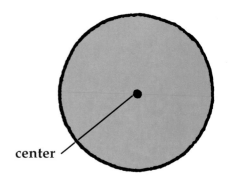

center

The circle has been an interesting shape for many thousands of years. It is the shape that influenced the invention of the wheel.

TO DO

Road signs are of different shapes. Some are circular. All circular road signs have a common meaning. Find out what this is.

There are many circular shapes in this picture. *How many can you see?*

An instrument for drawing circles is called a pair of compasses.

By moving the arms of the compasses but keeping the point fixed, you can use them to draw a whole set of circles which have the same center. These are called concentric circles.

If a circle is sliced exactly in half, then each half is called a semicircle. Some archways are semicircular.

TO DO

Draw a circle with thread and a pencil.
- Tie a piece of thread around a pencil.
- Tie the other end to a drawing pin.
- Place a piece of paper on a drawing board, fix the drawing pin, and draw your circle.

11 PARTS OF CIRCLES

The distance around the curved part of a circle is called its **circumference.**

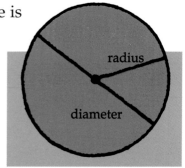

The length of the line that cuts the circle exactly in half, passing through the center is called its **diameter.** The distance from the center of the circle to any point on the boundary is called the **radius** of the circle. The radius is half the diameter.

radius

diameter

The circumference of a circle is about three times its diameter. So if you can measure the diameter of a wheel, multiply this by 3 to find the circumference of the wheel. This will tell you how far the bicycle will travel in one complete turn of the wheel.

TO DO

Measure the circumference of a coin by rolling it.

- Draw a straight line.
- Start by marking a point on the edge of the coin.
- Gently roll the coin along the straight line, noting the starting position of the mark on the coin.
- When this mark comes back to its starting position, stop rolling the coin.
- Mark the distance the coin has rolled along the line. This will be the circumference of the coin.

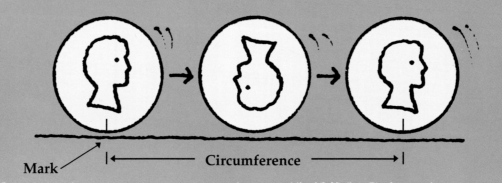

Mark

|← Circumference →|

Another way of measuring the circumference of a circle is to use some thread. For example, to find the circumference of the circular end of a lid from a jar, wrap a piece of thread around the lid. Then stretching the thread straight, measure its length with a ruler. This will be the circumference of the lid.

 CHALLENGE

Find a circular lid. Measure its diameter. Guess the circumference. Then use thread to measure the circumference to see how good your guess was.

Any straight line that joins two points on the circumference of a circle is called a **chord**. Chord comes from a Latin word meaning "string." A chord divides the circle into two **segments**. Any part of the circumference of the circle is called an **arc**. Arc comes from a Latin word meaning "bow."

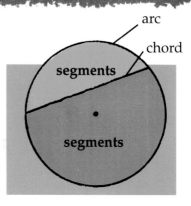

 TO DO

This circle has 4 points marked on it, which makes 4 arcs. When the points are joined, it is possible to draw 6 chords. Find out how many arcs and chords there are when the circle has 5 points.

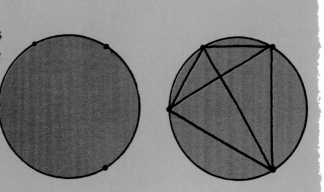

12 POLYHEDRA

A **polyhedron** is a solid three-dimensional shape with faces that are polygons. If we are talking about more than one polyhedron, we describe them as **polyhedra.**

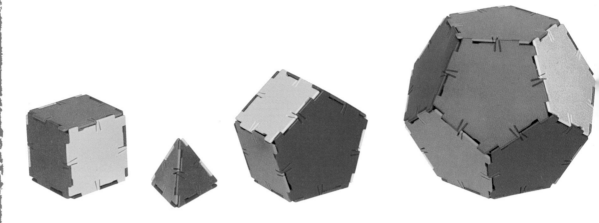

Here is a set of different polyhedra. Study the shapes of the faces. *Can you name some of them?* Polyhedra have special names based on their number of faces.

The best known polyhedra are listed in the factbox.

FACTBOX	
Name	**Faces**
Tetrahedron	4
Pentahedron	5
Hexahedron	6
Octahedron	8
Decahedron	10
Dodecahedron	12
Icosahedron	20

You will remember that two-dimensional shapes with straight sides are called polygons. We also saw that if all sides of a polygon are the same length, and all its angles are the same size, it is called a regular polygon.

If all the faces of a polyhedron are the same regular polygon, it is called a regular polyhedron. If not, it is called an irregular polyhedron.

There are only five regular polyhedra. They are:

- the regular **tetrahedron**, with 4 equilateral triangle faces
- the regular **hexahedron**, with 6 square faces (this is a cube)
- the regular **octahedron**, with 8 equilateral triangle faces
- the regular **dodecahedron**, with 12 pentagon faces
- the regular **icosahedron**, with 20 equilateral triangle faces.

CHALLENGE

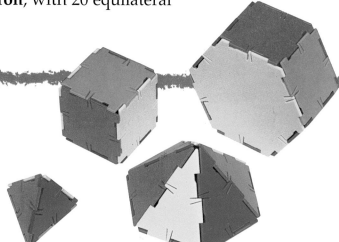

How many regular polyhedra are in this photograph? Can you name them?

Some polyhedra are beautiful to look at. You can make them by taking a piece of cardboard and drawing an outline of the joined faces on it. The outline is called a net. To make the polyhedron, cut out the net then score along the lines so that they will fold. Finally, glue the tabs to make your solid.

TO DO

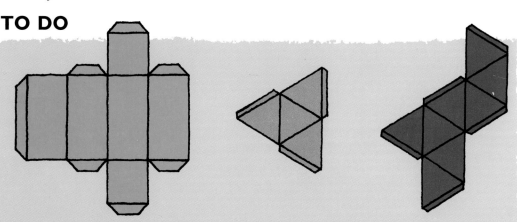

Can you imagine the shapes that can be made from these nets? Draw one of the nets on cardboard, then make the polyhedron.

13 CUBES

A **cube** is a three-dimensional shape.
It has 6 identical square faces.
It has 8 vertices and 12 edges.
If an object is shaped like a cube, we describe its shape as **cubic**.

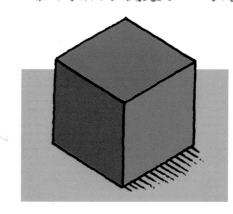

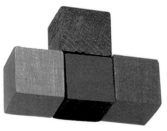

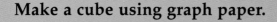

Toy building blocks are cubic because they fit neatly together, without leaving any gaps. Here are three different buildings made from four cubes.
Is it possible to make any more from four cubes?

TO DO

Make a cube using graph paper.

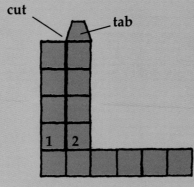

cut   tab

1 2

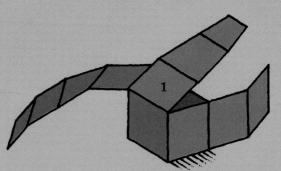

1

- Start by drawing this outline and cutting it out. Make the squares 2 inches long.
- Cut along the thick line, and crease the edges of the squares so that they fold the same way.
- Fold the 1-square over the 2-square.
- Continue folding, and finally tuck in the tab to make your cube.

The small cubes all have edges that are 1 inch long. They are called **cubic inches.** The open cube has edges that are 10 inches long. *How many cubic inches do you think can fit inside the open cube?*

CHALLENGE

Solve the inside-out puzzle.

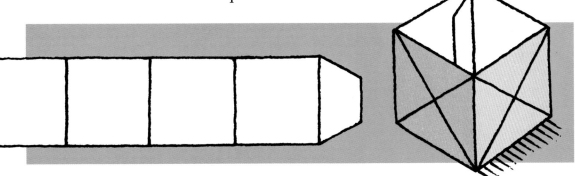

- Cut out a strip of four squares from thin white cardboard, with a tab at the end of one of the squares.
- Color one side of the strip.
- Now draw and fold along both diagonals of each square.
- Glue the tab to make a hollow cube, so that the colored faces are on the outside of the cube, and the white faces are on the inside.

To solve the puzzle, you need to turn the cube inside out, so that the colored faces are on the inside, and the white faces are on the outside. Don't force it; it can be done!

NETS OF CUBES

A net is a drawing that can be cut and folded to make a three-dimensional shape. Here is a net of a cube. It can be drawn with squares, cut out, then folded along the lines to make a cube shape.

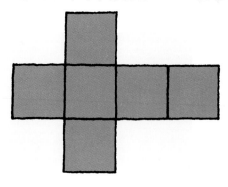

There are many different nets that will fold to make a cube. Here are four.

TO DO

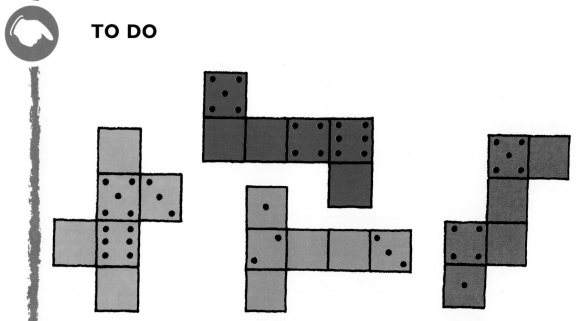

These are nets to make number cubes. The opposite faces of a number cube always have a total of 7 dots. Draw the nets, figure out the number of dots on the blank faces, then put them in your drawing.

Some of these twelve nets will build an open cube.
An open cube is a cube shape with one face missing.

How many of the nets will fold to make an open cube?

You can test them by making them with graph paper, then folding them.

TO DO

Make a cubic calendar.

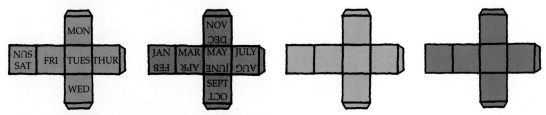

You need four cubes.
- On the faces of one cube, write the days of the week.
- On another cube, write two months on each face.
- Write numbers on two cubes to show the date.
- Put the four cubes together and the calendar will show the day, date, and month.

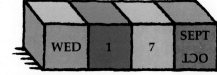

You will need to figure out how to number the two date cubes so that you can show every date in a month.

A **rectangular prism** is another three-dimensional shape. It has 6 rectangular faces.

A cube is a special rectangular prism in which all these faces are squares.

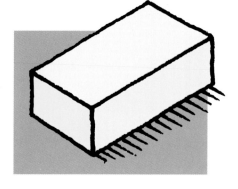

These boxes are rectangular prisms. The top and bottom have the same rectangle shape. The front and back also have the same shape. So do the two ends.

A solid with 6 faces is called a hexahedron. A rectangular prism is an example of a hexahedron. A cube is a regular hexahedron.

Many people live in apartment buildings. The building is often shaped like a rectangular prism, and so are the apartments.

You can see many rectangular prisms at the grocery store. It is the most common 3-dimensional shape.

These rectangular prisms have been built with cubes. *How many cubes are needed to make each one?*

Here is a summary of the properties of rectangular prisms.

FACTBOX				
Name	**Faces**	**Edges**	**Vertices**	**Shape of Faces**
Rect.Prism	8	12	8	Pairs of identical rectangles (could include squares)
Cube	8	12	8	Squares

CHALLENGE

With 24 blocks it is possible to build some differently shaped rectangular prisms. Here are two. Can you find four more?

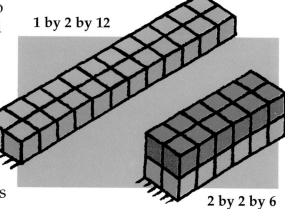

1 by 2 by 12

2 by 2 by 6

How many rectangular prisms can you build with 36 blocks?

16 PYRAMIDS

A **pyramid** is a shape with a pointed top and a flat base. Most pyramids have a flat base that is square-shaped. Because a square is a kind of rectangle, we call these rectangular pyramids. If the base is triangular, then the pyramid is called a triangular pyramid. Similarly, there are pentagonal pyramids, hexagonal pyramids, and so on.

The ancient stone pyramids in Egypt are examples of rectangular pyramids.

Here are some pyramids.
Which is triangular? Which is rectangular? Which is pentagonal? Which is hexagonal?

The sloping faces of all pyramids are triangular.
How many faces does each pyramid have?

34

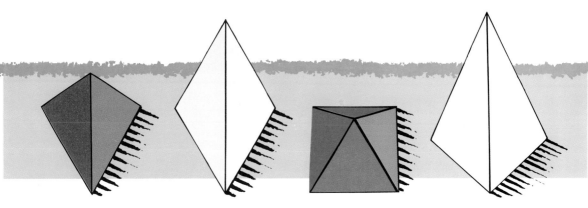

Look at the triangular faces of the pyramids. One of the rectangular pyramids has faces that are equilateral triangles, the other has faces that are isosceles triangles. The same is true for the two triangular pyramids.
As the size of the triangular faces becomes longer, the pyramid becomes taller.

TO DO

Make a rectangular pyramid from a net.

To draw the net:
Start by drawing an 3 inch square. Set a pair of compasses to 3 inches. Draw short arcs, with the compass point on each vertex of the square.

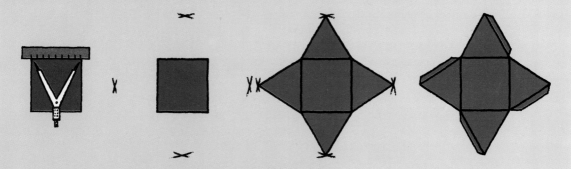

Draw lines from the vertices to the point where the arcs meet. Draw tabs along the four edges as shown. Cut out the net, score along the lines, fold, and glue the tabs.

CHALLENGE

Make two of these rectangular pyramids. Put them together to make a regular octahedron. Draw dots on the 8 faces to make a number cube.

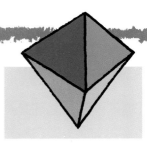

OTHER TYPES OF PRISMS

A **prism** is a three-dimensional solid that has the same shape at each end.

If the shape at each end is a triangle, the prism is called a triangular prism. If the shape at the end is a pentagon, the prism is called a pentagonal prism. If the shape at the end is a hexagon, the prism is called a hexagonal prism. All the sides, or faces of a prism are rectangles.

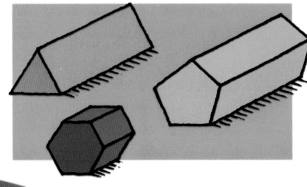

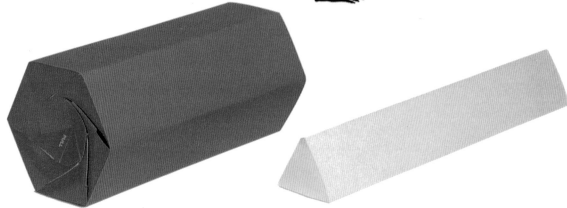

This is an example of a hexagonal prism and a triangular prism.

You have already seen rectangular prisms like this. It has the same shape at each end—a rectangle.

Are these boxes prisms? What sort of prisms are they?

Five of these six nets will make a prism. Which ones?

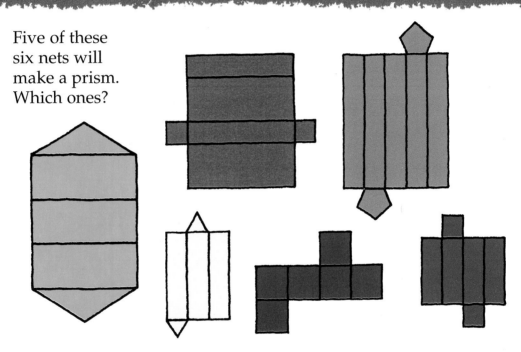

 TO DO

Make a triangular prism kaleidoscope.

- You need three rectangular mirrors, or shiny pieces of cardboard.
- Tape the mirrors, reflective side inward, to make a triangular prism.
- Cover one end of the prism with tracing paper.
- Place some small pieces of colored paper through the other end of the prism. What pattern can you see?

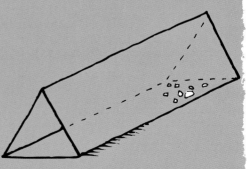

Try making some different patterns.

CONES AND CYLINDERS

A **cylinder** is a 3-dimensional solid with circles at each end. If an object is shaped like a cylinder, we say it is cylindrical.

Most pipes are cylindrical.

Which of these cans are cylindrical?

Cylinders are all around us.

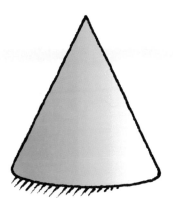

A **cone** has a circular base and a point at the top. If an object is shaped like a cone, we say it is conical.

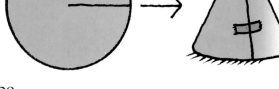

This lampshade is conical, but without the point. It is a part of a cone.

 TO DO

Make a cone from a sheet of paper.

- Start with a circular piece of paper.
- Draw a straight line from the center of the circle to the edge, and cut along the line.
- Curl the paper into a cone, and seal it with a piece of tape.

Can you make a cylinder from a rectangular sheet of paper?

CHALLENGE

There are four 3-dimensional shapes whose names begin with the letter "c."
Can you name them?

TETRAHEDRA

A triangular pyramid is called a **tetrahedron.**
If we are talking about more than one tetrahedron, we describe them as **tetrahedra**.

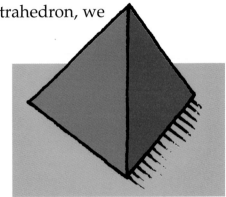

This regular tetrahedron has 4 faces that are identical equilateral triangles, meaning that all the triangles are the same size. This means that all the edges of the tetrahedron are the same length.

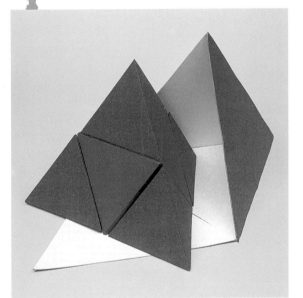

If you place four identical regular tetrahedra together with an octahedron with the same sized edge, they can be arranged to make a larger tetrahedron.

TO DO

Make a tetrahedron.

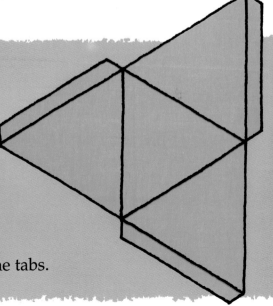

- You need an equilateral triangle template.
- Draw this net and tabs.
- Cut it out, score along the lines, fold, and glue the tabs.

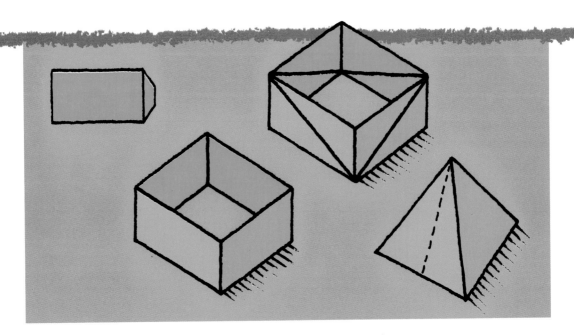

There are lots of other interesting ways to build tetrahedra. One way is to start with four 6 x 4 inch rectangles cut from cardboard, with a tab on one edge of each. The tabs are glued and joined to make a hollow box.

The diagonals are drawn as shown in the diagram, and good creases are made along the diagonals. Then the shape is folded to make a tetrahedron.

 ## CHALLENGE

Can you make a tetrahedron from an old envelope?

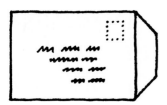  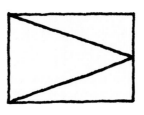 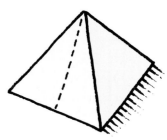

It is best to use a large brown envelope.
• Start by cutting across the envelope at the open end.
• Mark the mid-point of the open edge.
• Draw lines from here to the two opposite corners.
• Score and fold these lines firmly.
• Now hold up the envelope firmly, and blow into it.

20 SPHERES AND HEMISPHERES

A **sphere** is a perfectly rounded three-dimensional shape. It always looks the same from whatever direction you look at it. If an object is shaped like a sphere, it is described as **spherical.** It is different from most other three-dimensional shapes because it has just one curved face, and no vertices or edges.

A ball is a sphere. A billiard ball is perfectly rounded so it can roll in a neat straight line.

Many games and sports use spherical shapes.

The width of a sphere is called its diameter. To measure the diameter of a sphere, place two blocks firmly on either side of the sphere, then use a ruler to measure the distance between the two blocks. This will be the diameter of the sphere. The radius of the sphere, which is the distance from the center of the sphere to its surface, is half the diameter.

When a sphere is sliced in half, each half is called a **hemisphere**.

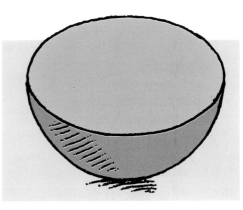

Many fruits are almost spherical. A hemisphere has a curved face and a flat circular face.

TO DO

Design and make an open box to hold four table tennis balls. Design one for six table tennis balls.

GLOSSARY

arc	Part of the boundary of a circle.
chord	A straight line that divides a circle into two pieces.
circumference	The distance around the boundary of a circle.
cone	A 3-D shape with a pointed top and a circular base.
cube	A rectangular prism whose faces are all squares.
cylinder	A prism with a circular face at each end.
decagon	A 10-sided polygon.
decahedron	A 10-faced polyhedron.
diameter	The length of a chord of a circle that passes through the center.
dodecahedron	A 12-faced polyhedron.
equilateral triangle	A triangle whose sides are all the same length.
hemisphere	Half a sphere.
heptagon	A 7-sided polygon.
hexagon	A 6-sided polygon.
irregular polygon	A polygon whose sides and angles are unequal.
isosceles triangle	A triangle that has two equal sides.
kite	A quadrilateral with two pairs of adjacent equal sides.
nonagon	A 9-sided polygon.
octagon	An 8-sided polygon.
octahedron	An 8-faced polyhedron.
parallel lines	Lines that if extended in both directions will never meet.
parallelogram	A quadrilateral with two pairs of opposite parallel sides.

pentagon	A 5-sided polygon.
pentahedron	A 5-faced polyhedron.
plane shape	Another name for a flat (2-D) shape.
polygon	A 2-D shape with straight sides.
polyhedron, polyhedra	A 3-D shape with faces that are polygons.
prism	A 3-D shape with an identical polygon face at each end, joined by rectangle faces.
pyramid	A 3-D shape with a pointed top and a flat base.
quadrilateral	A 4-sided polygon.
radius	The distance from the center of a circle to its boundary.
rectangle	A parallelogram with four right angles.
rectangular prism	A 6-faced polyhedron whose faces are rectangles; a "box" shape.
regular polygon	A polygon whose sides are all the same length and whose angles are all the same size.
rhombus	A parallelogram with four equal sides.
right triangle	A triangle that has a right angle.
scalene triangle	A triangle whose sides are all of different lengths.
segment	A piece of a circle cut off by a chord.
sphere	A perfectly rounded 3-D shape; a "ball" shape.
square	A rectangle with four equal sides.
tetrahedron, tetrahedra	A polyhedron with four triangular faces.
trapezoid	A quadrilateral with one pair of parallel sides.
triangle	A 3-sided polygon.
vertex, vertices	The corner of a shape (2-D or 3-D).

INDEX

angles	7, 10, 16, 26	parallelogram	16-18, 20
arc	10, 25	pentagon	4, 6, 27, 34, 36
chord	25		
circle	11, 22-25, 38-39	pentahedron	26
		polygon	6-7, 12, 17, 20, 26
circumference	24-25		
cone	38-39	polyhedron	26-27
cube	27-33	prism	36-37
		pyramid	5, 34-35, 39-40
cylinder	38-39		
decagon	6	quadrilateral	4, 6, 12, 14, 16-18, 20-21
decahedron	26		
diagonal	20, 29, 41	radius	24, 43
		rectangle	12-17, 20, 32-33, 36-37, 39, 41
diameter	24-25, 43		
dodecahedron	26-27	rectangular prisms	32-33, 36
equilateral triangle	10-11, 27, 35, 40	rhombus	17-18, 20
		right angle	10, 12, 14, 19-20
heptagon	6		
hexagon	4-5, 34, 36	right triangle	10
hexahedron	26-27, 32	scalene triangle	10
icosahedron	26-27	segment	25
isosceles triangle	10, 35	semicircle	23
kite	20	square	14-15, 17, 19-20, 27-30, 34-35
net	27, 30-31, 35, 37		
		tetrahedron	26-27, 40-41
nonagon	6	trapezoid	18-20
octagon	6		
octahedron	26-27, 35, 40	triangle	4, 6, 8-11, 20, 34-37, 40
parallel	16, 18-20	vertices	4-5, 28, 42

ANSWERS

p. 4	Rectangle, oval, pentagon, parallelogram. Quadrilateral: 4 sides, 4 vertices; pentagon: 5 sides, 5 vertices; hexagon: 6 sides, 6 vertices
p. 5	Shape 1: 8 vertices, 6 faces, 12 edges Shape 3: 6 vertices, 5 faces, 9 edges
p. 6	Hexagon, pentagon, quadrilateral, triangle
p. 7	Square

p. 9   **Challenge**

p. 11   Triangles - top row: right and isosceles, isosceles, right, right, and isosceles.
bottom row: isosceles, scalene, scalene, right, and isosceles

p. 12   **Challenge**
The tennis court has 9 rectangles.

p. 13   2 by 5, 5 by 3, 5 by 6, 3 by 6, 1 by 4

To Do

A few suggestions are:

p. 15   64 small squares

p. 17

p. 18   The shape at top center is not a trapezoid.

p. 19

p. 21 Challenge
top row - trapezoid, parallelogram, rectangle, kite
2nd row - quadrilateral, trapezoid, quadrilateral, square
3rd row - square, square, kite, trapezoid
bottom row - parallelogram, quadrilateral, kite, quadrilateral

p. 25 10 chords and 5 arcs

p. 26 The faces are square, triangle, and pentagon.

p. 27 **Challenge**
2 regular polyhedra - cube and tetrahedron.

To Do
Rectangular prism, tetrahedron, octahedron

p. 28

p. 29 1000 cubic inches

p. 30

p. 31

p. 33 12 cubes, 15 cubes, 24 cubes

Challenge
With 24 blocks you can build, 2 by 3 by 4; 1 by 3 by 8;
1 by 1 by 24; 1 by 4 by 6.
With 36 blocks you can build seven rectangular prisms:
1 by 1 by 36; 2 by 2 by 9; 1 by 2 by 18; 1 by 4 by 9;
1 by 3 by 12; 2 by 3 by 6; 1 by 6 by 6.

p. 34 The pyramids, from left to right are: triangular - 4;
pentagonal - 6 faces; hexagonal - 7 faces;
square based - 5 faces.

p. 37 Hexagonal prism, triangular prism, hexagonal prism

Challenge
The net on the left does not make a prism.

p. 38 The cylindrical cans are the two tomato soups and the
apple juice cans.